The Mother of the Bride

A PRACTICAL GUIDE & AN ELEGANT KEEPSAKE

The Mother of the Bride

A PRACTICAL GUIDE & AN ELEGANT KEEPSAKE

text by Marguerite Smolen
photography by Carol Ross

SELLERS
PUBLISHING

To Helen Levine, with love, for
being my mother of the bride, 1971.

Carol Ross

Published by Sellers Publishing, Inc.
So. Portland, Maine

Copyright 2004 © PM Design Group, Inc.
Photography 2004 © Carol Ross
www.carolrossphotography.com

Text by Marguerite Smolen

Series Editor: Robin Haywood
Production Editor: Mary Baldwin

P.O. Box 818, Portland, Maine 04104
For ordering information:
Toll free: (800) 625-3386 Fax: (207) 772-6814
Visit our Web site: www.sellerspublishing.com
E-mail: rsp@rsvp.com

ISBN: 978-1-56906-578-5
Library of Congress Control Number: 2004099907

Printed in China
Third Printing, August 2008

Contents

INTRODUCTION

As an editor involved in the bridal business for more than a decade, I've witnessed dozens of weddings and heard stories about hundreds more. I'm touched when I'm told by a couple how much the efforts of the mother of the bride helped to make their wedding a dream come true.

Society has changed a great deal during the last few decades. Social institutions, such as weddings, have changed, too. Many mothers find the kind of wedding celebration that appeals to today's couples, and, often, the circumstances in which it takes place, very different from those of their own. Consequently, they are unsure about what role they are supposed to play or how to proceed with the wedding planning process.

If you've picked up this book, you're probably a mother who wants to know how she can best help a daughter who is about to be married or you might be a bride-to-be who wants to acknowledge the important role her mother, stepmother, or yes, even her mother-in-law-to-be, plays in her life by providing her with the information she needs to help out. Either way, this book is meant to help ground you, the mother, as you negotiate the complexities that are involved in helping the affianced couple to realize their dreams.

Orchestrating a wedding, no matter how small, is no simple matter. There are a myriad of details to attend to. Legal matters must be resolved. Caterers and musicians should be booked, limousines hired, and tuxedo rentals arranged. And of course, there is shopping for the all important gown. Add to the mix family politics. Marriage is not just the merging of two people, but two — sometimes more — families, who may be of different cultures or traditions. It is also a social institution; traditionally, where friends and family of different backgrounds and ages are invited to witness a solemn commit-

ment. To deal with all of these variables, you almost need the expertise of a public relations firm, a psychologist, a party planner, a lawyer, and an embassy staff to boot.

Don't worry. As a mother, you've already honed many of the necessary skills you need to handle this task, and, moreover, you have an inside track on many of the parties involved. What you do need, though, is information. That's where this book comes in. Drawing from knowledge acquired while planning more than one hundred weddings, the following pages provide you with what you need to know to help your daughter and her husband-to-be plan this affair of the heart. Whether your daughter asks you to plan the whole thing or wants you to lend a hand on an emergency basis, you'll have the tools you need to succeed.

We've organized the book into four sections, each geared to tackle an important aspect of the wedding planning process.

Section 1 describes the roles and responsibilities that mothers of the brides are traditionally responsible for. It provides an overview of the entire process, including a wedding timeline.

This will enable you to orient yourself quickly, whether you are involved from the very beginning, or asked to lend a hand at key spots along the way.

As a mother, don't be surprised when your "grown-up" daughter turns to you for advice during the inevitable wedding crisis. Read Section 2, and you won't disappoint her in her hour of need.

For advice on how to look your best for this special occasion, turn to Section 3. Here you'll find tips on choosing a gown, makeup, and hairstyle that will enhance your natural attributes, express your individuality, and assure that you blend with the overall theme of the wedding.

Traditionally, the bride's parents host the wedding. When the affair is large, they may also host other special events, such as an engagement party, an after-wedding open house, or a next-day brunch. Even if the affair is not elaborate, you may find yourself hosting a smaller party for out-of-town guests or a bridal luncheon. Section 4, "Hosting in Style," includes party planning worksheets which will help you stay organized when planning an event, no matter what its size.

Before you know it, your daughter's wedding day will be here. Almost too soon for the effort that went into it, it will pass into memory, like so many other family weddings before it. Sadly, memories, however vibrant, often fade. But they don't have to. At the end of this book are pages to scrapbook your keepsakes, ensuring that your daughter's wedding will never be forgotten.

Marguerite Smolen

What Is My Role?

- Raising the Subject
- The Mother's Timeline
- What Style of Wedding?
- Budgets and Finances
- Announcing the Engagement
- Shopping for Wedding Attire
- Preparing Guest Lists and Invitations
- The Wedding Day
- At-A-Glance Wedding Timeline
- Dates to Remember

First and foremost, your chief role, as the mother of a bride, is to offer love, support, and understanding as your daughter defines herself anew as a married woman. Your daughter's life will soon change dramatically, and planning a celebration to mark that change, exciting and wonderful though it is, may spark moments of insecurity and stress. As her mom, you are well positioned to see your daughter through the emotional roller coaster that inevitably accompanies planning a wedding. If you respect your daughter's wishes and tastes, remain considerate of her needs, and offer to do some of the legwork for her, you will free her time. This will allow her to enjoy the process of planning her wedding more.

In times past, the mother of the bride was considered the official hostess of the event. The bride's family was expected to bear the burden of paying for the wedding. Consequently, the bride's mother orchestrated almost the entire affair, sometimes with the bride providing little to no input at all. Times have changed. Contemporary lifestyles have reduced the role that the bride's mother plays in all but the most traditional of weddings.

Many of today's couples have been living together for some time, or are older when they choose to get married. They may be on their second or third marriage. With increasing frequency, such couples are taking on the role of planning and paying for their weddings themselves.

Even when a mother plays a major role in organizing and financing the wedding, she rarely makes a decision without a great deal of input from the bride — and, sometimes, the groom. As the social roles of men and women have blurred, so too have their wedding duties. In today's equal partnerships, grooms are taking on more wedding planning responsibilities.

It's also more common today to find the groom's family helping out. Perhaps this is due in large part to the high cost of weddings in our culture. Never before has there been a generation so educated in the lifestyles of the rich and famous, or so many vendors willing to cater to those lifestyles. Young couples, many of whom have been raised on television shows that document celebrity weddings, have high, and perhaps unrealistic, expectations about how marriage should be celebrated.

Fifty years ago, sandwiches and punch in the church hall sufficed. Today, weddings are commonly held in banquet halls with elaborate catering packages that offer little room for

financial maneuvering. In addition, the rearranging of the "traditional" family also has impacted the picture. Single mothers may find the financial burden of a wedding beyond their means, and couples may lack the income to pay for their dream reception. In these cases, it is not unusual for the parties to pool their resources to create a celebration of some size.

Raising the Subject

You are about to be involved in the marriage of a contemporary young woman, someone who is very special to you, and you want to do whatever you can to help. Your role may not be as clear as your mother's may have been when you were married. Yet your goal remains the same — to help the couple you care about create the wedding of their dreams.

On the following pages, we'll discuss the responsibilities typically assigned to the mother of the bride throughout the planning process, on the day of the wedding, and functions following the wedding. We've created a timeline (see pp. 44-45) that will provide a quick at-a-glance look at what happens when. Keep in mind that, depending on the circumstances and your degree of involvement, your specific duties may vary.

The Mother's Timeline

Receiving News of the Engagement

You may suspect, but not know for sure, that your daughter is about to be engaged. Few grooms today follow the tradition of asking a father for a daughter's hand in marriage, and your daughter may not have confided with you, hoping to surprise you with the happy news. But once you've learned their intentions, it's important to let your daughter and future son-in-law know that you are there for them. When the couple announces their engagement, custom dictates that you congratulate them immediately. If the announcement takes place at a convenient place and time — for example, dinner at a restaurant — an impromptu gesture of celebration, such as ordering a bottle of champagne or sparkling wine, or dessert, will set a festive mood and underscore your positive acceptance of the news.

Once you've established a convivial atmosphere, touch on the subject of the upcoming wedding itself. Take it slowly at this point. You don't want to appear overbearing. For now, it's enough to suggest that you meet the groom's parents soon (if you haven't already), and discuss the best way to do so.

Meeting and Greeting the In-Laws

If you have never met your future son-in-law's parents, you will want to know whether they are married or divorced, and what is the best place and time for you to get together with them. You may ask the groom for telephone numbers or other contact information, following up with, "I'd love to invite your parents for dinner." If they are divorced, you can invite them separately for lunch, or for another activity

that might interest one of them: "I'd like to invite your father for a game of golf and your mother for lunch." If your daughter's future in-laws live at a distance, a friendly phone call or letter is a welcoming gesture. If you don't expect to meet for some time, you may want to send them a family picture as well.

As soon as possible, it's also important for you to begin forging ties with your future son-in-law. After all, he will soon be a member of your family. The best possible scenario is that you have known him for some time, but today,

with families living at a distance and children waiting to get married until they are older, it's not unusual for parents to have limited contact with their daughter's fiancé prior to marriage. If you do not already have his phone number or contact information, ask for it. Let him know you'd love to get to know him better and that you will call him soon to set up some private time. If you are married, and the groom and your husband share a common interest, your husband may invite him to an upcoming sporting event or a game of golf or racquetball at his sports club.

You know that your daughter is making one of the most important decisions of her life — a decision that will impact her in every respect — socially, financially, emotionally, psychologically, and physically. For now, however, try not to get too anxious about wedding plans, money, the possibility of grandchildren, or the other thousand worries and concerns you

may have about your daughter's future. An invitation at this point should be low-key, and simply an effort to get to know the future in-laws better.

Planning the Wedding and Reception — Establishing Your Role

After the initial social introductions have taken place, you'll want to establish what role you will play in your daughter's wedding. If time is of the essence, this subject may come up when the couple announces their engagement. If not, once you've had an opportunity to meet the in-laws (or if you already know them), it's appropriate to suggest a planning session to review the couple's needs and establish responsibilities.

With so much emotion surrounding this life event, it's often difficult for everyone involved to remember that the wedding celebration involves contracts, dates, and money, and therefore

is also a business activity. It may be easier for everyone to communicate needs and responsibilities if the planning session is held at a restaurant or other location that can be viewed by all as neutral territory.

Prior to this first planning session, you need to speak with your husband, if you are married (or your ex-husband, if you're on good terms), about what role you, as parents, should play, and whether you have any apprehensions about the upcoming event. For example, how much money do you have available to help finance the wedding? (The average wedding costs $28,000 today.) Do you have any contacts that can help ease the planning process, such as a friend who owns a Rolls Royce or has an "in" at a country club? The idea is not to plan the event at this time, but to agree with each other about what you can bring to the table. If you can work out your approach together and then present a united front when discussing the big event, the actual planning sessions will run more smoothly.

You may wish to meet with your daughter separately as well, before the first planning session, to get a general idea of what her expectations are. This might be a good time to take her to lunch. (In fact, plan periodic lunches with your daughter throughout the process, to remind her she has a life outside of work and the wedding!) If you are estranged from the bride's father, you will want to discuss up front what you can and cannot do and ask your daughter what her expectations are regarding her father's involvement. (See Section 2 for tips on dealing with divorce and stepfamilies.)

If your daughter does not already have a wedding organizer book (see Wedding Resources, p. 111, for suggestions), the two of you might shop for one now. It's a good idea to bring the organizer to the first meeting so

that there is a comprehensive and "objective" source for identifying wedding planning responsibilities. Also refer to Section 4 of this book, "Hosting in Style," where you'll find a party planning worksheet that provides an overview of the many details involved in planning a large event. If both sets of parents are to be involved, make sure paper and pens are on hand so everyone can make their "To-do" lists.

If you expect to head up or otherwise be extensively involved in the planning process, you may want to bring a three-ring-notebook or a binder so you can keep your notes organized right from the start. At the end of this section, you'll find an At-A-Glance Wedding Timeline. This convenient chart provides a quick look at "what to do when" over the course of a year. If your planning time is shorter, use the chart as a guideline and condense tasks as necessary.

Following the timeline is the Dates to Remember chart that provides the basic tasks of organizing a typical wedding as they might occur over the course of a year. Space is provided for you to note the tasks that have been assigned to you. For clarity, you may wish to settle on some written method (short of a contract) of recording everyone's tasks. This will help to eliminate any confusion about who's doing what in the months ahead. Before the first planning session ends, be sure to schedule the next planning session and establish a method — e-mail, telephone, newsletter — for keeping everyone up to date on the wedding plans.

What Style of Wedding?

Formal or informal? Large or small? Before or during the first planning session, you need to clarify the couple's preferred approach to their wedding and plan to accommodate their wishes as best you can. Knowing from the outset whether the couple prefers a wedding that is small or large, casual or elaborate, with a sleek, urban look or a country theme is important for many reasons.

Should you be asked to contribute financially to the wedding, you will want to get a sense of what the couple's dream wedding could cost. Typically, the largest expenditure of the wedding budget is the reception cost.

As the bride's mother, you will be expected to run interference with friends and family members who may expect to receive an invitation for the big event. The style of the wedding is an important indicator of the number of guests who can be invited. What portion of the guest list will be set aside for the couple's friends? How many of the parents' friends and family members will be invited? What will the total number of guests be?

In the likelihood that you are being asked to host this event, the wedding

style will give you an idea of your options for getting some help. If they prefer a small wedding, perhaps you can host the reception at your house and plan to do the catering yourself. This involves planning a menu, buying and possibly cooking the food (having the event catered would be easier on you), setting up a bar or punch table, and possibly borrowing or renting chairs, tables, china, glasses, cutlery, and decorations. It will also most likely involve some redecorating, new landscaping and house cleaning. If many people are to be accommodated, you may have to rent a tent and dance floor. Typically, an at-home wedding does not save much money, time, or effort. A better solution might be to rent a room in a local restaurant and offer guests a prix-fixe meal.

If the wedding is of moderate size,

Who Pays for What?

Although there's plenty of wiggle room in the financial responsibilities assigned various family members in the course of planning today's weddings, for those who wish to follow tradition, or at least use the traditional breakdown of who pays for what, here are guidelines:

THE BRIDE'S FAMILY: Engagement party • invitations and announcements, including postage costs • church fees • the cost to transport the bridal party from the bride's house to the ceremony and between the ceremony location to the reception • bride's wedding attire, including headpiece, shoes, gloves, and accessories • bridesmaids' bouquets, and for large, formal weddings, attendants' dresses, if they cannot afford to purchase the required gown • mother- and father-of-the-bride's attire • grandmothers' corsages • birdseed shower • flowers for the ceremony and reception • decorative props and other rentals for the ceremony and reception, such as aisle runner, chuppah, candelabras, tents, latticework arches, columns,

(continued on next page)

and held at a banquet hall or other catering establishment, you may be able to enlist the assistance of an in-house planner, but be prepared to sacrifice some freedom of choice — they most likely will have a pre-selected list of contacts that they do business with. If the wedding is to be large and elaborate, consider talking to the couple about enlisting the aid of an independent wedding planner whose job is to custom design an entirely unique affair.

Last, but not least, it's never too early to start working on your own look for the big day, which should fit into the overall theme of the wedding. (See Section 3, p. 71, for suggestions and guidance.)

Budgets and Finances

Use the initial planning session to confirm your role, financial and otherwise, by having a frank discussion with your

daughter and son-in-law-to-be about expectations. This will go a long way to avoid misunderstandings, hurt, disappointments, and other stresses later on. It's in everyone's best interest to be as clear as possible. Discuss what lies ahead and who's paying for what. It helps to be prepared with some typical wedding costs in your geographic area. Ask the bride if it's okay for you to research some costs prior to the planning session, so that you can all arrive at a realistic budget (at least in general). If the wedding is being held in your hometown, the local librarian can help you to locate a newspaper wedding supplement which should list prices,. You can also call or visit a catering hall (they rarely provide prices over

chairs and tables • the reception itself, including programs, location, food, drinks, caterer, favors, chairs and tables • photography, videography, music for the ceremony and reception • transportation of the bridal party • favors, for instance, napkins and matches printed with the couple's name and wedding date • the wedding cake • lodging for out-of-town attendants, and, sometimes, guests • a generous gift to the couple upon their marriage • bridal shower • after-the-ceremony wedding brunch or open house.

THE BRIDE: Groom's wedding ring and gift • gifts for bridesmaids, female attendant, flower girls and ringbearers • her own medical checkup and blood test.

THE GROOM: The marriage license • clergy or officiant fee • his attire • gloves and other fashion accessories for the groomsmen and ushers • bride's bouquet, wedding ring, and gift • mothers' corsages • boutonnieres for himself and male

(continued on next page)

(continued from previous page)

attendants • gifts for best man, grooms-men, and ushers • his own medical visit and blood test • transportation from the wedding to the honeymoon • accommodations for his out-of-town attendants • honeymoon.

THE GROOM'S FAMILY: Their own clothes • the rehearsal dinner • often, bar and liquor at the reception.

BRIDAL ATTENDANTS: Their own travel expenses • their own attire • bachelorette party • gifts for the couple.

BEST MAN AND GROOMSMEN OR USHERS: Their own travel expenses • their own attire • bachelor party • gifts for the couple.

GUESTS AND ATTENDANTS: Their own travel expenses • gifts for the couple.

the phone) to find out what a typical package in your area consists of. If the wedding is being held away, you may have to be more creative, asking a friend or neighbor in the area to help out.

Confirm up front what the couple's expectations are regarding traditional mother-of-the-bride duties, especially the primary ones of hosting the reception, organizing receiving lines, arranging for transportation, and managing the other tasks outlined on the following pages of this book.

The couple may tell you, right from the start, that they wish to take care of planning the entire wedding themselves, either with or without your financial support. If the couple intends to organize the wedding themselves, smile as graciously as you can and let them know you'll be happy to help them out. Don't be surprised if they come running for assistance in the near future! Better still, check in with them periodically to see how they're doing.

take over, though — or risk having the charge of being a bossy MOB (the industry code word for mother of the bride) levied at you.

If several people are contributing financially to the wedding, it may make sense to open a separate bank account for the purpose of paying for the wedding. All of the concerned parties can then deposit their funds into this account, and the checkbook can be given to the couple for use in paying for expenses.

If you are expected to pay for the event, it's only natural that you should wonder how the couple is going to spend your money. You may also need some reassurance that they will not overspend. Keep in mind, though, that your daughter and her fiancé are adults, and their spending habits, for better or worse, are pretty ingrained by now. Although you should defer decisions regarding the style and flavor of the wedding to the couple, if you

Give them the opportunity to ask for your help.

Take care of party planning details well in advance. It will reduce stress for everyone. Rein in any attempt to

DISPLAYING THE WEDDING GIFTS

According to traditional wedding ettiquette, wedding gifts may be received once the wedding has been announced, after the invitations have been sent out, and even after the actual wedding has taken place.

Traditionally, wedding gifts were sent to the bride's home (i.e., the home of her parents). A room was designated to display the bride's gifts. You may offer to have the wedding gifts delivered to your home, where you can keep a record (perhaps on a computer spreadsheet) of who sent what, making it easier to assemble and print out a list of who should receive thank-you notes and for what gift.

are paying for the wedding, you will probably be more heavily involved in fine-tuning the budget and contracting with vendors. Section 4 of this book can help you rough out a budget. For planning tips and negotiating strategies, see Section 2: "Etiquette and Other Matters," which includes advice about how to deal with people and prevent and deal with disasters, such as budget overruns or other events that may impact the money set aside for the celebration.

Announcing the Engagement

In the Newspaper and Magazines

Traditionally, the mother of the bride arranges for a formal picture of her daughter (or the couple) to appear in the local newspaper, along with the announcement. Call the newspaper's local lifestyle or society page editorial department and ask the editor what the policy is. Most local newspapers will send you a standard form to use for this announcement. In the typical published announcement, the bride's parents announce the engagement of their daughter, her maiden name, the name of the groom, the names of both parents, their occupations, and a few sentences about the couple's schooling or career achievements, plus the month and year in which the couple plans to hold their wedding. Mail in the completed form with a head shot, a good quality portrait taken by a professional photographer, such as the kind taken at high school or college graduation (minus the cap and gown), is appropriate. If you do not have one, you may arrange for your daughter or the couple to sit for an engagement portrait at a local photography studio. Do not send the newspaper a life-sized, framed portrait! A frameless photo is the only kind that can be scanned, and the closer the photo is to the size that will appear in the newspaper, the better. Some newspapers may also accept scanned digital images from CD-ROMs.

The lead time needed by a newspaper to run a wedding announcement varies, depending on whether the newspaper is a daily or weekly. When you call, ask the editor when, approximately, you can expect to see it run. Announcements in the newspaper, however, are never guaranteed to run on a specific date because available space will change depending on advertising pages and late-breaking stories. Therefore, you may have to monitor several issues before you see news of the engagement in print.

Getting the announcement of a couple's engagement, or photographs of their wedding portrait or recep-tion, in a magazine is more complicat-ed. Today there are many magazines, national and regional, that publish details of weddings in their pages. However, this coverage is typically limited to celebrities or families of some local social standing. If there is something unusual about the upcom-ing wedding — that it has a unique theme (Renaissance fair or Civil War,

era) — or that it was beautifully produced on a shoestring, or took place in another country, you can, if you wish, write a letter of inquiry describing the event in as much detail as possible, and send it to an editor with "scouting" photos (photos taken prior to the event that will give the editor an idea of potential photo opportunities). Your story may spark the interest of an editor who will want to pursue the story, either with the magazine's own photographer or yours (if the photos turn out to be good enough). Don't expect a story of this kind to run for months, or possibly even a year down the road. Magazines typically work three months to a year in advance of publication.

The Engagement Party

The parents of the bride customarily host the engagement party for friends and family. The purpose of the party is

Making Hotel Reservations for Out-of-Town Guests

If the bride's family has invited out-of-town guests to the wedding, reserving their accommodations is the responsibility of the mother of the bride. The mother of the groom is responsible for reservations for out-of-town guests invited by the groom's family. In times past, out-of-town guests would be put up at the home of the parents or those of other family and friends. Today, guests stay at hotels. Usually you can ensure guests a discount if you reserve a block of rooms well in advance of the wedding date. You might also try a small inn or a bed and breakfast, but reserve early to ensure accommodations.

Guests are generally expected to pay for their own rooms (unless they cannot afford to do so, in which case the family may offer to pay).

to formally transition your daughter's fiancé into the family's social circle and welcome him into the family. The engagement party can be large or small, casual or fancy. It can suggest the formality of the upcoming celebration, or it can announce the upcoming nuptials in a more casual manner, or it can be a prelude to a fancier event. As the hostess, you decide the scope of the party. (For party planning details, see Section 4.)

Shopping for Wedding Attire

One of the most cherished of wedding traditions for many mothers and daughters is shopping for the wedding gown. The mother usually accompanies the bride in her search for the perfect dress, accessories, and trousseau and she may help to choose the bridesmaids' dresses. The bride's attire, however, is the focus of the initial forays into bridal salons. Let the bride lead the way, but don't hesitate to be honest with her if she asks for your opinion about what brings out the beauty of her eyes, hair, or figure.

As the bride draws closer to selecting her gown, the look and style of the wedding will begin to come into focus. At this point, you can begin to consider your own gown options. During your gown shopping process, stay in close contact with the mother of the groom. Traditionally, the mother of

The Day Before the Wedding

The mother of the bride's house is often location central the day before a wedding. Traditionally, the bride gets dressed at her mother's house, along with her bridesmaids. Often, the mother may host out-of-town guests, or be in the final stages of preparation for an open house to follow the wedding reception. Plan to take the day off from work, and to arise early. A nice touch is to take household members out to breakfast, so you don't have to cook and can review any last-minute details in a calm atmosphere. You may wish to designate someone to make final calls about the wedding, accept last-minute gifts sent to the house, order take-out, accept flower deliveries, and talk to the caterers if you are preparing to host an affair after the reception.

You might decide to follow breakfast with a trip to the beauty salon, so you can look your best during the day ahead, which will culminate in the rehearsal and, afterward, the rehearsal dinner. (Remember to book this appointment three to four months in advance to ensure your appointment is secure.)

the bride chooses her dress before the groom's mother chooses hers. Both of the mother's gowns should be different, but complementary in color and style. For advice on selecting a gown and how to ensure you look your best, see Section 3.

The father of the bride's attire should echo the formality of the groom's and his ushers and may be rented if he does not own suitable formalwear.

Preparing Guest Lists and Invitations

Traditionally, the bride's mother acts as her daughter's social secretary during the wedding planning process, helping to prepare guest lists, to write and

mail invitations, and to keep track of acceptances and refusals (expect between 10 and 20 percent, depending on the time of year). You may help the bride select her invitations, although the style of invitation is up to the bride.

Depending on your agreement with your daughter, you may be involved in compiling the guest list and gathering mailing addresses. The guest list is usually comprised of friends and family from both sides, as well as friends of the couple. It's helpful to establish early on (during the budgeting process when the size of the wedding is determined) how many people each side can invite.

The data you assemble during the process of compiling the invitation list will form the basis of the reception seating plan (which you may help to finalize about a week prior to the wedding), the thank-you's sent by the couple after the wedding, and the invitations to numerous smaller affairs that typically occur before and after a wedding, such as the bridal shower and post-wedding open house.

Managing the guest list for a large wedding takes some skill; the use of a computer spreadsheet is recommended to keep track of invitations sent and replies received, as well as the numerous Web sites available. If you are not computer-savvy, you can rely on a Rolodex or address book purchased for the ocassion. As regrets come in, there may be room to invite additional guests.

Rehearsals

The Ceremony Rehearsal

Since wedding ceremony sites frequently have more than one event booked a weekend during popular months, they often group wedding rehearsals together on a single evening (often it's a Friday night). Ensuring that everyone arrives at the location in a timely fashion is therefore important.

You can help out by offering to organize transportation for family members on the bride's side to ensure they arrive promptly. A good approach is to have everyone gather at a central location — your house at a designated time — to review logistics for the evening and the next day. Maps and directions can be provided, cabs hired, limos booked, or, if necessary a family member can be assigned chauffeuring duties to pick up and deliver key people. At the rehearsal, you will practice entering and leaving the ceremony site, as well as any other part you may play in the ceremony. This is also the day to review the seating plan and confirm any special touches that have been planned.

The Rehearsal Dinner

The rehearsal dinner is hosted by the groom's parents. It can be a casual, at-home affair or a more elaborate event in a fine restaurant. The only caveat is

that everyone who plays a part in the ceremony must be invited, as well as the spouse or significant other of those participating, and the parents of any children in the wedding.

During the rehearsal dinner, the father of the bride traditionally toasts the couple. As mother of the bride, you can briefly remind everyone of last-minute details, such as where to stand in the receiving line and who will take home any miscellaneous items (candles, extra programs, flowers). Try to keep the business part of the rehearsal dinner brief. This is the mother of the groom's time to shine!

The Wedding Day

The morning of the wedding, in addition to attending to your own appearance, your primary job is to assist the bride — offer her emotional support, help to soothe her anxiety, and deal with last-minute emergencies (see Section 2, pp. 62-65).

Now is the time to say those heartfelt words to your daughter about the meaning of marriage and your love for her. If you have not already done so, this is also a good time to give your daughter a special treasure to remind her of this wonderful day. Silverware or jewelry are two popular choices, along with a family heirloom — but,

if you are talented at a craft, your gift from mother to daughter may be something you've made, such as a quilt, sampler, framed wedding invitation decorated with quilling, ornamental marriage certificate, decorative family tree, or an album of family photographs — something your daughter will treasure for decades to come.

Your doorbell continues to ring as the bridesmaids and the wedding party flowers arrive, along with the hairdresser (if you have booked an at-home service), and the photographer. An often-requested photo is that of the mother helping her daughter to get dressed. Photos are traditionally then taken with other close family members, including the groom's parents. The day of the wedding, you should get dressed early so you can be on hand for these photographs.

or horse-and-carriage, as the case may be). The mother of the bride travels separately. In advance of the wedding, make plans for your own transportation. Enlist a relative to drive you, or perhaps hire another limousine for you, the parents of the groom, or other family members to share, or, if you are married to someone other than the bride's father, the bride's stepfather, assuming he's invited.

Seating and Escorts

The groom and the groom's parents should arrive at the ceremony site about one hour before the scheduled time for the ceremony. They will most likely convene in a small side room until the actual ceremony time.

Weddings today have become more creative than ever. Contemporary couples seek to make their weddings a personal statement, and they often need

Transportation to the Ceremony

Finally, the time comes to leave for the ceremony site. The bridesmaids usually ride together in a limousine. The father and the bride travel together in a separate limousine (or antique car,

to accommodate stepfamilies or other nontraditional family situations (for more about this subject, see Section 2). But most weddings incorporate some conventional wedding protocol. The groom's mother walks down the aisle, escorted by an usher, or her son, the groom, to the first row on the right-hand side, with her husband following behind. (If the parents are divorced, the father of the groom will already be seated, two rows behind the groom's mother's row.)

The mother of the bride leaves her home for the ceremony about ten min-utes prior to her daughter's departure. She is escorted down the aisle by an usher or one of her sons, if he is in the wedding party. She is the last to be seated, — after the parents of the groom. She sits in the first row on the left-hand side, in the end seat on the center aisle. The seating of the mother of the bride signals that the bridal procession and the ceremony will begin momentarily, and no one may be seated after she is. Together with the groom's mother, the mother of the bride may light a family candle on the altar, after the candle lighters have left the altar area, and prior to the entrance of the wedding party. During the ceremony, the mother may be asked to do a reading. If there is no maid of honor, the mother of the bride takes charge of the bride's bouquet during the service.

After the register is signed, the recessional takes place and the mother of the bride returns the bouquet to her daughter. The bride and groom leave the place of worship first, followed by the bridesmaids escorted by the ushers. The mother of the bride exits next, escorted by an usher, with her husband following. The last in the party to leave is the mother of the groom, escorted by an usher with her husband following.

The Reception

If this is a traditional wedding, and the bride's parents have paid for and organized the wedding, the mother of the bride acts as the hostess of the wedding reception. She stands at

the entrance to the reception with the mother of the groom, greeting guests as they enter, while the father of the bride and the father of the groom circulate. Just behind the two mothers is the official receiving line, which traditionally is limited to the wedding party minus the best man and the ushers. The bride stands to the groom's right and the maid of honor stands on the bride's right. Half of the bridesmaids (if they are included) stand on one side of the bride and half stand on the other (or follow to the right of the maid of honor).

In many of today's weddings, though, the traditional rules of the receiving line are ignored because the families enjoy having the parents included in the receiving line. In such cases, the mother of the bride stands next to the father of the groom, followed by the mother of the groom, the father of the bride, and then the couple, followed by the bridesmaids.

At casual weddings, the receiving line is often dispensed with altogether. However, since its purpose is to welcome guests and meet and greet family and friends from both sides, if you opt not to have one, everyone in the wedding party should make it a point to circulate among the guests to make introductions.

AFTER-THE-WEDDING PARTIES

There is nothing like a wedding to put people in a party atmosphere and, as one of the big life events, motivate them to connect with long-lost friends and family. It's almost become de rigueur to host an open house immediately after a reception at the home of the bride's parents or a brunch for close family and friends the next day, especially for those out-of-town guests who may have booked hotel rooms. The party planner in Section 4 can help you prepare for such an event. Even if you do not have a formal party, you may discover that people plan to come by to see the wedding gifts and talk over the wedding.

In a more formal wedding, the receiving line is maintained until all of the guests have been seated. Then, the emcee announces the names of the wedding party and, beginning with the newly married couple, the bridal party takes to the dance floor.

As mother of the bride, you will dance with the groom immediately after he has had his first dance with the bride. The bride will dance at the same time with her father. Afterward, you are free to dance with your husband and then anyone else who solicits an entry on your dance card.

The mother of the bride is traditionally seated at the parent's table to the left of the father of the groom and opposite the father of the bride, who sits with the mother of the groom to his left.

At the end of the party, the mother of the bride sees the couple off with everyone else. The mother of the bride usually is the last to leave the reception. If she has been the chief wed-

ding planner, she'll need to settle any outstanding bills (or delegate someone else to do so), bring home gifts, leftover favors, flowers, pastries, and any remaining cake (packaged by the caterers), along with the cake topper. In smaller halls, she may be responsible for making sure everything is tidied up before leaving. However, if the mother of the bride is planning an after-the-reception open house, she may wish to enlist help with these matters or ask a friend or relative to perform the final check so she can arrive home before her guests do.

AT-A-GLANCE WEDDING TIMELINE

This chart provides a quick overview of the major tasks associated with planning a wedding and what happens when. Keep in mind that, depending on your degree of involvement, your specific duties may vary.

TO-DO TIMELINE	MONTH 1	MONTH 2	MONTH 3	MONTH 4	MONTH 5	MONTH 6
Announce engagement		✓				
Prepare budget						
Set the date	✓					
Select venue	✓					
Meet with officiant	✓					
Determine guest list						
Select wedding party		✓				
Register for gifts						
Book photographer		✓				
Book musicians/DJ		✓				
Book florist						✓
Book videographer		✓				
Plan rehearsal dinner						
Select invitations				✓		
Plan/book honeymoon						
Book hotels for guests						
Arrange transportation						
Select gown						
Select wedding rings						
Finalize guest list						
Select menu, bar & cake	✓					
Mail invitations						
Prepare ceremony prog.						
Buy wedding party gifts						
Get marriage license & BT						
Look for place to live						
Prepare seating plan						
Pack for honeymoon						
Send thank-you notes						

MONTH 7	MONTH 8	MONTH 9	MONTH 10	MONTH 11	MONTH 12
✓					
✓					
				✓	
	✓				
		✓			
		✓			
	✓		✓		
				✓	
				✓	
				✓	
				✓	
				✓	
	✓				
					✓
					✓
					✓

DATES TO REMEMBER

This chart outlines the basic tasks of organizing a typical wedding as it might occur over the course of a year. Space is provided for you to note and organize the tasks that have been assigned to you.

TO-DO TIMELINE	MONTH 1	MONTH 2	MONTH 3	MONTH 4	MONTH 5	MONTH 6
Announce the Engagement						
Attend Wedding Planning Meeting						
Obtain Wedding Party, Groom, and Groom's Parents Names and Contact Information *(Home and Work Addresses, E-mail, Cell and Home Phones)*						
Meet with Officiant						
Book Ceremony Site *(Note Dimensions, Bathroom Locations, Dressing Room Availability, Lighting) Time Distance to Walk Down the Aisle, Take Scouting Shots for Florist and Photographer.*						
Book Reception Hall *(Note Dimensions, Ask for Seating Chart, Bathroom Locations, Dance Floor Size, Dressing Rooms, Lighting.) Take Scouting Shots for Florist and Photographer.*						

MONTH 7	MONTH 8	MONTH 9	MONTH 10	MONTH 11	MONTH 12

DATES TO REMEMBER

TO-DO TIMELINE	MONTH 1	MONTH 2	MONTH 3	MONTH 4	MONTH 5	MONTH 6
Select Wedding Party						
Book a Photographer						
Book a Videographer						
Hire Musicians for the Ceremony						
Hire Musicians for the Reception						
Shop for Wedding Attire						
Decorate/Landscape House						
My Beauty Routine and Fitness Services						
Rent Props, Extra Seating, Decorations						
Order Invitations and Announcements						
Complete Guest List						
Hire a Florist (Bring Bridesmaids' Gown Color Swatches)						
Shop for Wedding Cake						
Order Liquor						

MONTH 7	MONTH 8	MONTH 9	MONTH 10	MONTH 11	MONTH 12

DATES TO REMEMBER

TO-DO TIMELINE	MONTH 1	MONTH 2	MONTH 3	MONTH 4	MONTH 5	MONTH 6
Shop for Wedding Favors						
Shop for the Gift Registry						
Plan a Bridesmaid's Shower						
Purchase Gifts and Favors						
Host Party for Out-of-Town Guests						
Do a "Dry Run" to Time Distances Between Locations						
Create Wedding-Day Timetables						
Book Housecleaner						
Book Babysitter/ Pet Sitter						
Attend Rehearsal Dinner						
Host an After-the-Wedding Party						
Other						

MONTH 7	MONTH 8	MONTH 9	MONTH 10	MONTH 11	MONTH 12

Etiquette and Other Matters

Questions & Answers Concerning:

Divorced Parents

Older and Younger Party Guests

Children and the Wedding

Interfaith Marriage

The Pregnant Bride

Choice of Groom

How to Add Your Special Touch

Bending the Rules

Preventing Problems and Dealing
  with Emergencies

Dealing with a Stressed-Out Bride

Saving Money on Reception Costs

Relatives Who Are Ill

Honoring a Dead Parent

Calling Off a Wedding

Your daughter counts on you for sound advice. Whether you are orchestrating the entire wedding, providing emotional support, or are regarded by the bride as someone to "bounce" thoughts and ideas off, it helps to know how to handle some of the sticky situations that can arise while planning a wedding.

The following questions and answers will help prepare you for most of the common — and some of the uncommon — problem wedding scenarios. Don't get too frazzled, though. The better prepared you are, the less likely it is that anything bad will occur. Few weddings run as smoothly as we'd like, and many of the "disasters" that occur become, in time, moments to remember.

In theory, it shouldn't. Both parents, no matter how acrimonious they feel toward each other, should stifle their resentment, hurt, and disappointment with each other so their child is able to enjoy this special time.

The reality is that parents can sometimes feel overwhelmed by unpleasant emotions that have been left over from the demise of their own marriage. Unresolved feelings are difficult to control in times of stress, and planning a wedding can certainly qualify as a stressful time.

To get through this difficult situation, decide that you will control your emotions rather than allowing your emotions to control you. Begin by taking the best care of yourself that you

possibly can. That may include practicing deep breathing, meditation, and/or prayer daily; exercising regularly; reducing other commitments so you get enough sleep; eating properly; scheduling regular sessions with an aesthetician and massage therapist — whatever you need to do to control stress.

Can you rely on your daughter to act as an intermediary between you and your husband? Perhaps she or another sibling is already accustomed to performing this function. If the bride and groom are paying for the wedding themselves, or if a bank account has been set up to fund the wedding, there may be little need for any kind of mediation between you and your ex. Your child will simply convey details about time, attire, and roles to each of you separately, and you will follow through accordingly.

If you are the chief wedding organizer, and you think that things might

get a bit tricky, or if you prefer not to burden your child with the role of go-between, consider hiring a wedding planner. Alternatively, you might consider asking a neutral family member to convey information back and forth or suggest how duties could be fairly distributed so that both the bride's biological father and stepfather, for instance, feel recognized and involved.

There are established etiquette rules for dealing with separation, divorce, and remarriage on the actual day of the wedding. If the parents aren't actually divorced, they should issue the wedding invitation and host the ceremony and reception as if they were happily married. Neither should attend the wedding with a "friend" because they are, no matter how long they have been separated, still married.

If a parent has remarried, he or she may attend the wedding with their current spouse. The stepfather sits beside his wife, who is the mother of either the bride or groom, in the first row. The birth father and his current spouse sit in the second or third row behind them. If relations are friendly, stepparents may attend the reception as guests if the bride requests it. Otherwise, the birth parent may attend alone as an important guest.

If the parents are divorced, whoever gives the reception acts as host or hostess along with his or her current spouse (if he or she is remarried). For example, if the mother has remarried and throws the reception with her new husband, they "receive" the guests, and the bride's father may attend as a guest. The same would be true the other way around: if the father throws the reception, his current wife acts as hostess and the bride's mother is a guest.

If neither parent has remarried, they may, if they can put aside their differences for this special day, stand together to receive the guests.

Divorced parents, and their new spouses, are not expected to sit together at a parents' table.

We are inviting some older family members to the wedding, but my daughter's heart is set on a rock band. How can I convince her to book a band that will appeal to people of all ages?

Most wedding bands and deejays are used to playing a variety of music, including standards that appeal to people of any age, even if they're a rock 'n' roll or hip-hop band. You might ask the band to start out playing slower music and segue into more of the club-style music, possibly when elderly relatives have departed for home. You can also alternate a band that appeals to a more youthful audience with musicians who will play less funky or instrumental music between sets. Or you could have jazz or classical music during the cocktail hour and popular music during the wedding reception.

Keep in mind, though, that the wedding day is a celebration of your daughter and new son-in-law; therefore, they should be allowed to choose band music that appeals to them. Besides, many middle-aged and older people enjoy the energy that comes with a more youthful sound.

Do we have to invite children to the wedding?

No, it is not a requirement to invite children to a wedding; however, some parents of young children turn down the invitation or leave early if they can't bring their children.

An alternative is to arrange for the children to be taken care of and entertained elsewhere — in a nearby room at the hotel or at a relative's house, with babysitters in attendance, of course!

If this is a second marriage, it is a good idea for the children to attend both the wedding and reception, because the ritual and celebration will help to make them feel a part of the new family that is being created. You might also engage a clergy person who will help craft a wedding ceremony that incorporates the children.

My daughter was raised in the United States, but she is marrying someone from another faith/country. What do I do?

There are many books on interfaith and ethnic weddings that provide valuable advice to mothers in your situation. Also, an increasing number of clergy are practiced in performing interfaith ceremonies. Find one who can advise you on the best way to handle your specific circumstance.

If, however, the couple has decided to get married in a Western-style house of worship or civil wedding and have a typical reception, you may wish to ask your caterer to provide food that is in keeping with the groom's family's customary diet. For example, if the groom is from India, you can ask that Indian cuisine be served. But do ask your daughter's soon-to-be in-laws what the proper diet is — the population of India, for example, enjoys diverse cuisines and has different religious dietary restrictions. Some Indians are vegetarian, while others are not. If the groom's family is Jewish, you may need to arrange for kosher food to be served.

How should we celebrate the wedding of our pregnant daughter?

In times past, if the pregnancy was discovered early enough and kept secret, the wedding was celebrated with all of the customary trappings as if there were no pregnancy. Today, out-of-wedlock pregnancy is much more

common. Some couples wait until after the birth of the child to get married. Others prefer to get married in a civil or religious ceremony while the bride is pregnant and wait a year or so to hold a larger celebratory party. Ultimately, this is a matter of personal choice on part of the bride and groom.

We think our daughter is making a mistake by marrying this particular person, but she is not to be dissuaded. How can we best handle this situation?

The truth is that this is an unfortunate problem for a large number of families. There are measures you can take to lessen potential damage and to support good healthy relationships with your daughter and future son-in-law. If there is a particular issue that concerns you such as a prior contentious divorce, a problem with employment, or a large debt, and the couple assure you that they acknowledge the problem and are working together to find a solution, then the best idea is probably to trust your daughter and accept her choice.

I'd like to honor the newly married couple by adding my own special touch to the celebration.

There may be a creative way for you to add something extra special to the event. Perhaps you have a talent for flower design; you can make some floral arrangements. If you can cook or make candy, you might make boxes of sweets for the guests to take away at the end of the evening. Are you good at ceramics? Perhaps you can design the wedding cake topper. If you are an amateur historian or journalist, the bride might appreciate your documenting the wedding planning process in a photo album. Or, maybe your interest lies in genealogy. If so, you can display a family tree or pictures of ancestor's weddings at the entrance to

the wedding reception. You could offer to pay for costumed dancers or strolling musicians that represent part of your ethnic heritage to play for a short time at the cocktail hour. If the wedding is being held at a historic house or unusual location, where the bathroom facilities are minimal, you could decorate some baskets and fill them with "necessary" luxuries, such as hand cream, special soaps, and towels, and place them on the bathroom counter for guests to use.

How important is it to follow traditional wedding etiquette as it's described in etiquette books?

Etiquette was developed out of a need to make people feel comfortable and welcome. If the bride and groom wish to depart from some of the formally scribed rules, or to create some new ones, they are still within the bounds of good taste if their decision is considerate of others and makes people feel at ease.

I have heard of several weddings that did not go well because of an unexpected disaster. How can I ensure everything will run smoothly on my daughter's wedding day?

The best hope you have of preventing wedding day disasters is to plan ahead. The better organized you are, the less opportunity there will be for something to go wrong. Here are several suggestions you can use as the planning proceeds:

• Keep copies of all receipts and
  written communications in a
  folder so that you can refer
  to them easily.

• Keep in touch with all participants
  and vendors on a regular basis to
  review your expectations and their
  schedules. Provide all wedding
  party members and vendors, such
  as photographers and musicians,
  with a list of previously agreed-
  upon duties, a customized
  timetable, a map, and directions —
  all on paper. Mail these information
  packets out a week before the wedding and follow up with a phone
  call to be sure that the packets
  arrived and were opened.

• Order extra boutonnieres in case
  one or more gets lost or crushed.

(continued on next page)

- Prepare silk flower arrangements in case the bride's bouquet or an attendant's bouquet gets crushed. (You can use them as decorations in your home if they're not needed.) Bring along extra floral wire, wire pins, and corsage pins, in case the original floral arrangement can be saved.

- If you opted for a seamstress to sew a gown and you have not had a final fitting at least two weeks before the wedding, assume the dress will not arrive in time. Shop for a back-up dress immediately.

- Watch the weather and lay in a supply of inexpensive umbrellas for guests to use in case of rain.

- Have an alternative location or a tent with sides if you plan an outdoor wedding.

- Check noise and parking ordinances in advance.

- Delay the serving of alcohol until after the toasts. Shut the

bar down early if it appears
drinking is getting out of hand.

- Have several disposable cameras
for candid shots, and in case the
photographer doesn't show.

And just in case something does
go terribly wrong,

- Buy wedding insurance.

Create the following emergency
kit, and keep it nearby throughout
the day of the wedding. Include
in the kit: Aspirin, Ibuprofen,
Tylenol, antacid tablets, smelling
salts, antihistamine tablets; safety
pins, thread in various colors,
scissors, sewing pins and needles,
tape, glue; tampons and sanitary
napkins; tissues; extra panty hose;
ballet or folding slippers for aching
feet; earring backs; hand wipes;
extra pens and paper; makeup;
toothbrush and toothpaste, den-
tal floss, mouthwash, and breath
mints; eye drops; deodorant; hair
brush and comb, hairspray; bobby
pins and hair bands; nail file and
polish (for both runs and nails);
tweezers; razor; a first-aid kit; flash-
light; static cling and de-wrinkling
spray; hand steamer; hand mirror;
batteries; film; sun block; hand
cream; protein bars; dry crackers;
bottled water.

Ever since we started to plan her wedding, my lovely daughter has turned into "Bridezilla." How can I best handle this?

Follow the rules for dealing with any stressed-out personality:

- Set boundaries.

- Listen before speaking.

- Practice compassionate detachment.

- Affirm that you love and care for the person.

- Wait a day to call back someone who has angered you.

- Allow the other person some space.

- Be willing to compromise.

- Communicate frequently.

- Spend time together bonding outside of organizing the event.

- Find out what it will take to get the other person's "buy-in."

- Put agreements in writing.

DON'T FORGET

All of the above rules can be overruled by the Super Rule that applies specifically to weddings:

- When in doubt, defer to the bride.

Do you have any tips for saving money on reception costs?

Plan to hold the reception at a time of the year (or day of the week) when reception halls are typically not busy, such as January or a Sunday morning. Reduce the number of musicians in the band, or allow them to take more frequent breaks or to play for a shorter period of time. Eliminate the open bar

at the reception and serve a sparkling wine toast instead with a cash bar. Make it a wedding breakfast, brunch, lunch, or tea rather than dinner. Reduce the number of guests by eliminating anyone you haven't seen in a year, people at work with whom the bride does not socialize, children (spell it out on the invitations). Print the invitations yourself on your home computer using blank cards from an office supply store.

The bride's aunt is in a rehabilitation center after suffering a minor heart ailment and can't attend the wedding. How can we make her feel included?

Collect wedding ephemera — program, napkins imprinted with the couple's wedding date, menu card, favors, and photographs — and deliver them to the aunt with a handwritten note saying how much she means to everyone.

The bride's father died of leukemia. How can we remember him?

One way is to ask guests through word of mouth, prior to the event, to donate money to a charity, such as the Leukemia Society, in lieu of a gift.

How do we call off the wedding?

If the engagement has been announced in the newspaper, follow up with a short notice stating that you and your husband announce that your daughter and her former fiancé have mutually agreed to end their engagement, or that the marriage will not take place. If the announcement is made just prior to the wedding, you must spread the news via the telephone. If a death in the family or other event prevents the wedding from taking place as planned, send an announcement regretting that the marriage will not take place as planned and stating that the ceremony will be held privately in the presence of the immediate family.

Your Wedding-Day Look

- Choosing Wedding Attire
- Flattering Your Figure
- Self-Care
- Polishing Your Look

Naturally, as you meet and greet family and friends on this special occasion, you want to look your best. You can start thinking about what to wear when you accompany the bride on her shopping trips to find her gown. However, it's usually best to wait until the bride has chosen her dress and those of her attendants before you shop seriously for yourself. There is no need for the mothers' outfits to match those of the attendants, since they are not official members of the bridal party. But the attire of the mother of the bride, as the wedding's official hostess, and the mother of the groom, as her honored guest, should complement the overall color scheme and style of the wedding.

Choosing Wedding Attire

More than almost anything else, wedding fashion tends to reflect social trends and attitudes. With the dramatic cultural changes that have occurred in the past half-century, "mother of the bride" no longer automatically translates into "dowdy matron." Today's mother tends to be fitter and have a younger attitude than her counterpart may have in decades past, and fashion has followed suit. "Official" mother-of-the-bride looks today range from conservative two-piece suits to sleek, beaded gowns with revealing silhouettes.

For many mothers, the enormity of options makes finding an outfit that strikes the right balance — not too young (after all, you don't want to look as if you're trying to compete with the bride!), but not too old

either — a challenge. A good plan is to begin with some general notion of what the wedding itself calls for and then see what options will best flatter your figure and coloring.

Who Chooses First — the Mother of the Bride or the Mother of the Groom?

The mother of the bride customarily chooses her gown first, followed by the mother of the groom, who should select a gown that coordinates in color and styling with the mother of the bride's gown. Although that's the custom, miscommunication between mothers has been known to happen.

To avoid a potentially awkward social situation, it helps to address the topic soon after the wedding has been announced, early in the planning stages. This is easy to do at the time the bride announces her colors and wedding style. You can establish what color you prefer to wear and then let the groom's mother suggest a complementary color for herself. You can discuss whether both of you will wear long gowns or street-length dresses, or one a gown or dress and the other a pantsuit. Then you can discuss possible fabrics. Armed with the answers to these questions, both mothers can start shopping for outfits that suit their figures and personalities.

If the Wedding is Scheduled for the Morning, Afternoon, or Evening...

Even at an elegant suburban restaurant, a backless evening gown looks out of place at 10 a.m. A wedding held in the morning or afternoon calls for a dress, suit, or pantsuit, unless the event is theme-driven. A Renaissance- or Victorian-themed wedding, for example, calls for a long gown. For an evening wedding, you can choose between a short dress, pantsuit, or a long gown, depending on its styling.

Formal or Casual?

Although we call long gowns "formal," the length of a dress does not necessarily indicate its formality, especially today when so many designers are working with asymmetrical hemlines and creating elegant suits. Much more indicative of the formality of a dress is the fabric. Silk, satin, velvet, and chiffon, and synthetic fabrics that imitate them, are considered formal fabrics. Cotton, rayon, and most knit fabrics are considered more casual, although trim, such as sparkling rhinestones, satin banding, or embroidery, such as soutache, can dress them up a bit.

Urban or Rural?

The décor and location of the ceremony and reception sites can help you choose an appropriately styled gown. Just use your common sense. Delicate fabrics and sweeping hems or flying scarves may be lovely if you are attending a wedding held in a contemporary hotel ballroom, where the environment is closed to dirt and thunderstorms. On the other hand, if the wedding is being held outdoors, you should consider a shorter dress or gown. Gowns with fishtail hems or sweep trains, which sometime show up in formalwear departments, can easily get dirty when walking across lawns. Since fabric-covered shoes are also susceptible to grass stains, it makes sense to wear leather for an outdoor wedding, perhaps in a dark color, or to do as ballroom dancers do — bring your fancy shoes in shoe bags and slip them on just prior to your formal entrance.

What's the Color Palette?

For decades, mothers were steered toward blue and pink when choosing their gowns. Such restrictions do not exist today. Even the age-old taboo of wearing black to a wedding has relaxed. Just about any color can be worn, as long as it works with the palette chosen by the bride and does not compete with the bride's gown. You can get inspiration from the colors in the flower arrangements, or from the bridesmaids' gowns. Consider a shade lighter or darker, or a neutral shade, such as beige. Keep in mind that all colors get a new lift with metallic or iridescent fabrics and add subtle glamour.

Mother-of-the-Bride Gown Trends

Suits: Dressing in two separate pieces — a jacket with either a skirt or pants, is a stand-out look for MOBs and is flattering for almost all figure types. Look for jackets with elegant features such as beading, embroidery, or sequin accents.

Off the Shoulder: Sleeveless, tank, or spaghetti straps (especially if you want to show off well-toned arms and shoulders) can be ideal. A must-have accessory is a lightweight wrap of cashmere or silk often sold with the dress, but it can be purchased separately and dyed to match. Also keep in mind sheer jackets cut in a classic style or metallic cardigans worn over a shimmery dress.

Flattering Your Figure

When you go shopping, wear appropriate foundation garments — there's little chance you'll be wearing an exercise bra under a formal evening gown, so opt for something more structured when you shop! You may want to visit a lingerie store first to get advice on undergarments that will enhance your "assets" and minimize any "flaws," as well as ensure that you're wearing correctly sized lingerie.

Also bring a pair of shoes similar in style and height to those you plan to wear. You may buy new undergarments or shoes once you actually find the gown, but those you wear while shopping can help you decide whether a particular style is realistic for you.

As you try on gowns in available styles and from various manufacturers, get a sense of how well they suit your body type. Examine them in a three-way mirror, if possible, and use a hand-

held mirror to see what's going on behind. Is the waist too long or short? Are armholes loose enough so you can raise your arms on the dance floor or pull them forward to hold a bouquet? Does the bodice pull or gather in horizontal folds across the back? Is the neck too tight? Is your chest uncomfortably exposed? Does the skirt bunch or drop smoothly over your hips and down?

High-priced models excepted (and even they will say otherwise) — no one has a perfect figure. Here are some tips to help you make the most of yours:

- Make a list of your assets and look for a gown that plays up most of them. For example, if you have beautiful shoulders, show them off. A collar, decorative neckline or trim, portrait neckline, or fanciful necklace and large earrings can help frame a beautiful face and smile and draw the eye away from a full middle.

- Simple sheaths or pantsuits in a monochromatic color scheme elongate the body and flatter both petite and plus-sized women. The trick is to get a sheath that hugs your curves. Often sheaths are not proportional to a woman's body, and sag and gap where you least want them to. A bias-cut fabric with some give can make the difference.

- A- or princess-line silhouettes flatter almost everyone.

- Long sleeves can help to elongate a silhouette, but may require hemming.

- If you have small shoulders, extend them with a puffed sleeve or decorative detail.

- Basque waists, which drop to a "V" in the front, as well as "V" necks, help elongate the body, but can make shorter women appear top heavy.

(continued on next page)

- Halter necklines can make you look bottom heavy, especially if you have narrow shoulders.

- If you have bony wrists or a prominent collarbone, go for some coverage, rather than choosing short sleeves and a scooped or off-the-shoulder neckline.

- Bolero jackets are often flattering to a petite frame, while jackets that fall just below the hips can help elongate a high waist (but be careful — they can cause you to look top heavy, too).

- Horizontal banding and beading widens whatever part of the body it's applied to, and can be great or awful on a pear-shaped silhouette. Used sparingly, it can balance you out — apply it at the shoulders if they are narrow, or at the hem to emphasize a full skirt and bell-shaped silhouette.

- Vertical trim or asymmetrical pleats, ruffles, or bands applied on an angle is more universally appealing.

- Voluminous amounts of gathered fabric, along with dropped waists, look good on few people. Tall, willowy, fine-boned women are the exception.

- Those who do not have near-perfect skin and firm muscles may want to avoid strapless styles or opt for covering exposed arms, shoulders, necklines, and/or backs with chiffon-like fabrics or a jacket.

Off-the-Rack vs. Special-Order Gowns

Start shopping in plenty of time — at least six months before the wedding. If money is an issue, you may find an outfit at an end-of-season sale, outlet store, or an upscale resale shop.

Many department stores carry mother-of-the-bride dresses, and they can be purchased off the rack. This is the simplest and easiest way to procure a gown because you know exactly what you are getting and presumably are buying a gown that fits well. If you fall in love with a particular style and decide to order your outfit from a special-occasion boutique, absolutely count on it taking up to 12 weeks to come in.

Horror stories abound of mothers ordering gowns over the Internet or having them custom-made by a local seamstress, only to discover that the dress doesn't arrive in time for the

wedding or is not the correct size, does not fit or hang properly, or is in some other way not wearable. You may get lucky, but don't count on it.

To avoid last-minute trauma, place your order *well in advance* of the wedding and order only from a source recommended by someone you know and whose judgment you value. Otherwise, buy your gown off-the-rack.

Alterations: Once your special-order gown arrives (and even if you purchase a dress or pantsuit off-the-rack), you will almost certainly need the hem adjusted. Manufacturers typically cut gowns and pants to accommodate tall women in high heels, figuring that the average-to-short woman can always have the item shortened. Wear the undergarments and shoes you've selected for the actual gown to your fittings. Most likely you will stand on a round, raised platform, so the tailor can make sure the hem is at the correct

length for the shoes you are wearing and that the hem hangs evenly all the way around.

For formal gowns, the hem should come to rest at the top of your toes; it should not fold over onto the shoe or be so high that large portions of the top of your foot are visible. If you are wearing a shorter dress, ask the tailor to help you decide what length is most flattering to your legs.

Verify that the tailor will sew the hem using a blind stitch that won't show, not a visible running machine stitch often found on jeans. If this occurs, there may not be enough hem to have it redone with a blind stitch. Covering the running stitch with a piece of lace or other trim may be your only solution.

If the available tailors are booked with other jobs, simply getting your dress hemmed may take a couple of weeks. Plan early and leave yourself plenty of time. Other alterations will only add to the delay.

Generally, it's not advisable to buy a gown with heavy beading, lace appliqué, or embroidery, and plan on alterations because the ornamentation is applied over the seams and taking the dress in will require ripping it apart and reapplying the beadwork or trim — a painstaking process that an average tailor may not have the skill, time, or patience for.

Cleaning and pressing: Having the gown handled by others, including tailors, prior to the wedding, increases the chance that the gown will have something spilled on it or wrinkle. Unfortunately, dry cleaning solvents may dissolve beading and can sometimes stain or discolor fabrics, such as silk. If this happens, you are back to square one, since, even if the dry cleaner offers to pay you some money,

you will still be without a gown. If something does happen, try a heavy dose, and, if necessary, multiple doses of club soda blotted with a clean, white cloth to remove spots. Wrinkles are best removed with a steamer. You can easily buy a handheld steamer from department or discount stores, or rent a commercial one. If these methods fail, look for a cleaner who specializes in bridal gowns and make sure you outline any concerns you have before handing over the gown.

Plan to have the dress altered and hanging in your closet a minimum of three weeks prior to the big day. If your special-order or altered dress has not arrived by then, start shopping for an alternative outfit to purchase off-the-rack. You do not want to leave the decision of what to wear to the last minute. Practically all that is available to you then is what your closet currently holds.

Self-Care

To some extent, your gown options may be limited by your physique because many more clothing options tend to be available to slim, rather than overweight, women. In any case, perhaps you've been meaning to lose a few extra pounds. If so, you are not alone. Many women — brides, mothers, and attendants alike — regard an upcoming wedding as an opportunity to make some changes in their physical appearance and polish their everyday look. If you are among them, you may wish to start a self-care plan of diet and exercise before you shop for that gown. Consider:

• Visiting your doctor to establish a baseline against which you can map your fitness results.

(continued on next page)

- Booking a personal trainer for a few sessions to get you started on an exercise program. Make sure your program includes a mix of aerobic, weight training, and flexibility exercises.

- Visiting a nutritionist for a more healthy and balanced diet.

- Keeping a record of your food intake and weight loss progress.

- Instead of going on a diet per se, cutting back on portion sizes.

- Eliminating one or two unhealthy foods that you routinely eat. Allow yourself to eat them as a treat once a month.

- Adding at least a half hour of exercise to your schedule each day — first thing in the morning, so you won't neglect to do it.

- Seeing to it that you get adequate amounts of water, sleep, and calcium — lack of these has been known to affect proper metabolism.

- Scheduling a few minutes of meditation first thing in the day, along with weekly, bi-weekly, or monthly spa services, to help you relieve stress.

- Reading or recording positive affirmations — enhancing your interior self positively affects your exterior self.

Polishing Your Look

To complete your wedding-day look, it's important to remember the finishing touches that can pull it all together. It's equally important to give yourself time to find the hairstyle or color change you want, the perfect makeup for both the wedding and photographs, to address your nails, and to perfectly accessorize with shoes and jewelry. The following are useful tips to help achieve that special look.

Hair and Makeup: If you plan to make significant changes to your hairstyle or undergo a series of facial treatments, such as any of the minimally invasive laser treatments or chemical peels, visit your aesthetician as soon as possible. These things take time. For example, growing out your hair will take several months, and some laser treatments are best done in the winter when the skin

tends to be less exposed to the sun. Since skin treatments and hair coloring can cause adverse reactions, don't plan any in the week or two before the wedding. Instead, plan a trial run of your new look at least two months before the day of the wedding. At this time, you should also book any hairstyling or makeup services for the day of or the day prior to the wedding.

Most salons have professional makeup artists who can customize your look, and beauty counters will also provide a makeup palette suitable to your skin tone. It helps to have a swatch of your gown, so the makeup artist can work with the color the gown will cast onto your skin.

Keep in mind that you will most likely want your makeup to last all day and look good in photos as well. This may require a heavier makeup application or a different color palette than you are used to. Professional makeup

artists create a natural look for the camera by sculpting the face with neutral browns and beiges, and set the look with powder. Once the makeup artist is finished, you can test what you look like by photographing yourself with a Polaroid or digital camera.

Nails: Pedicures last significantly longer than manicures. You can easily book a pedicure a week or two prior to the wedding, but you'll want to book your manicure the day before or the morning of. Since manicures can sometimes chip within a day, ask for a

bottle of nail polish in the same color as that applied, in case you need to touch up the polish. You can also make manicures and pedicures last longer by applying a clear nail hardener or topcoat on a daily basis. Acrylic nails, where the nail is filed down and a false tip is glued into the end and then filled with a solution and painted, are not for everyone, but you may wish to try them out for this special occasion. They will last from a few days up to a month, provided you do not use your hands a lot. They also take some getting used to; you may want to opt for the "sport" length if you're not used to having long nails. They come in a French manicure style that looks somewhat natural.

Shoes: Shoes can add an elegant touch to the simplest of outfits. Although very high heels are considered sexy, they are difficult to stand in for long hours. Opt instead for a low heel, perhaps one with a feminine, curvy "Louis" heel. Avoid mules because they'll inevitably slide off when you're dancing. If your shoes aren't well-padded, especially in key areas like the ball of the foot, you can pad them yourself with purchased "stick-on" inserts. Keep in mind, though, that because these inserts do take up some space, you may need a roomier shoe. You can bring some with you to try (make sure not to peel off the paper so they don't stick!).

Jewelry: If your dress is elaborate, keep jewelry to a minimum. A pair of simple earrings is all you need. Conversely, if your dress is understated, you may want one dazzling pair of earrings (and necklace) to complete your look. If you are unsure how to accessorize, study pictures in style magazines to see what does and doesn't work. Today, you can find jewelry in almost any style at any budget level.

- Party/Event Ideas
- Planning the Event
- Money Matters
- Party Planning Worksheet

Tears, laughter, and joy inevitably accompany the announcement of a couple's engagement. But the excitement soon becomes tempered by the realization that celebrating this important milestone takes a lot of work. Sadly, many who feel exhilarated at the start of the planning process wind up feeling exhausted and overwhelmed at the end. How disappointing, especially when, with the right kind of information and a little planning, an event can be a wonderful experience for guests and planners alike. To ensure that your celebration runs smoothly, consult the Party Planning Worksheet on page 102. It will help you stay focused and keep track of the dozens of details that go into making your event a resounding success.

Party/Event Ideas

A wedding often calls for additional celebrations of varying sizes. As an involved mother, you may find yourself being the party planner not just for the weddding ceremony and reception, but also for a number of other events. Here are some traditional party ideas, as well as some you may not have thought of:

Father/daughter "together" time:
Suggest to your husband that he and the bride take some special time together before the big day to celebrate dad's role in raising his daughter. They could meet for an activity that the two of them enjoy, such as going out to breakfast or playing a round of golf. Maybe your daughter could present her father with a gift that symbolizes their relationship: a special book that has meaning for both of them or a framed picture of her when she was a child. This is a great way for father and daughter to bond and create a memory that will live with each of them.

Mother/daughter/sister weekend:
What a fun idea to bring the bride's "chief assistants" together, get some planning done for the wedding, and

have fun at the same time! If your daughter lives in another city or state, plan a weekend where you and the bride's sisters can visit for a girls-only getaway of cooking, making wedding day favors, or even knitting bridal party gifts. The aim is to relax and enjoy your time together.

Pre-wedding bridal party get-together: Invite the bride's wedding party (her bridesmaids) to brunch, a day at a spa, or a day-cruise to create camaraderie and thank them for their help with the upcoming event.

Engagement party: Announce the upcoming nuptials and introduce the fiancé to family and friends with a small catered affair, picnic, or party in your house.

Bridal shower: The aim of this party is to help the bride and groom set up housekeeping by providing gifts of basic household items. In times past, the shower was an afternoon party held at the house of the bride's best friend and was attended only by women who were close to the bride and about her age. Now this

Party Games and Activities

Bridal showers are perfect opportunities for party games. They can be bridal-theme versions of just about any game, such as Pin the Tail on the Donkey (Pin the Train on the Bride), trivia (prizes can be wooden spoons and other inexpensive kitchen items if the shower is a kitchen-themed one, or spa goodies if it's an all-female shower); bridal bingo, etc.

Creating a scrapbook during the shower is a brilliant activity that will preserve lifelong memories for the bride and groom. Ask each guest to bring a memento that represents an experience they shared with the couple, a trip they took together, or an aspect of their personality (such as they both love tennis). Then have a large scrapbook on hand with decorations purchased from a crafts or stationery store, scissors, and glue, and ask each guest to create a page in the book. If the couple wishes, they can display the book at the wedding, along with photos of the bride and groom in their younger years.

event has expanded to include family members and guests of all ages (note — it's common courtesy to invite all shower guests to the wedding as well). Sometimes, the bride's mother hosts the event. These days, it's not uncommon to hold a "couples" shower, attended by both the bride and groom and their friends, male and female.

Sometimes a theme shower is held in lieu of, or together with, a general-purpose shower (that is, guests are asked to address a theme with an inexpensive token while still bringing a

regular gift of their choosing). Some popular themes are the round-the-clock shower, where each guest is assigned a specific hour of the day and told to bring a present associated with it (for example, a guest might bring an alarm clock if she were assigned the seven a.m. time slot, which is when most people get up); the cook's shower, where each guest contributes a recipe to a recipe box or a cooking utensil; the room-by-room shower, where each guest brings an item appropriate to a specific room in the house; or lingerie, garden, hobby, and home handyman showers.

A gathering of new in-laws:
Facilitate the first meeting between the parents of the bride and the parents of the groom by inviting the two families to dinner, cocktails, or another meal, such as brunch.

THE BRIDAL LUNCHEON

Inviting the bridesmaids, as well as your daughter, to lunch is a great way to get to know them better, as well as a nice "thank you" for all of the time and, yes, money they are spending on the wedding. If you are the primary organizer, the bridesmaid's luncheon can be an opportunity to firm up wedding plans, smooth the way for planning the bridal shower, or enlist recruits to help you out with all of the details.

Rehearsal dinner:

Relax after the wedding rehearsal — traditionally held on the evening before the wedding — at a dinner held at a restaurant. Take the opportunity to thank the wedding party for their support and assistance and to deliver last-minute instructions for the following day.

Open house:

Open your house during the downtime between ceremony and reception or after the reception to make out-of-town guests feel welcome and to catch up with friends or family members you haven't seen in awhile.

Mom and dad getaway:

Take time to thank your spouse for his help with the wedding, rekindle the romance of your own nuptials, and provide a mini-respite for yourself so you can return to planning the upcoming affair with renewed energy.

THE BRIDAL SHOWER

The bride's mother may host and pay for the bridal shower. If the bride's friends or another relative offers to host this event, offer your assistance. But, again, make sure tasks and responsibilities, including financial ones, are clearly outlined. I have heard of at least one mother who accepted bridesmaids' offer to host the engagement party with unhappy results. The bridesmaids organized the event without the mother's input, invited a large crowd to an expensive restaurant and, without warning, presented the mother with a bill totaling thousands!

Planning the Event

Whether you are hosting a wedding in the traditional mother-of-the-bride role, or another event related to the big one, good planning is essential.

Follow these steps on the next page to ensure that your special occasion is exactly the way you want it.

Step 1: Define the event

First, what is the purpose of the event (bridal shower, wedding reception)? Will it be formal or informal? How many people will attend? What type of people are they (male only or female only, mixed ages, relatives only, a mix of friends, family, and strangers, etc.)? When will it be held?

Step 2: Decide on a budget

How much money can you realistically spend on this event? Your budget will impact many decisions, such as the number of people you can invite and where you might hold the event. There's no simple way to establish a definite budget if the affair is to be a large one. For some tips on how to estimate costs, see the following pages.

Step 3: Work out the details

Once you know how much you can spend, and the approximate number of people you plan to invite, you can

begin to bid the project out to various vendors. You'll need to do some research to find out what catering and banquet facilities are available in your area or, if you are having an at-home event, who can cater your affair or supply you with party trays (one suggestion is to visit your local supermarket deli area).

Money Matters

To arrive at an initial budget, one approach is to estimate the total amount of dollars you have at your disposal and then assign a certain percentage of that total to various cost areas. As a general rule of thumb, here are some approximate percentages used by party planners:

- Invitations (including printing and postage), placecards, and other printed matter — 5%

- Special occasion clothing and accessories (purchased and rented) — 15%

- Food and site costs — 45%

- Alcohol and servers — 10%

- Entertainment — 10%

- Flowers — 5%

- Photography — 8%

- Other (transportation, keepsakes, gifts) — 2%

Sample Scenario #1

Add up the amount set aside for costs associated directly with guests, such as the food and alcohol costs, and divide that amount by party size to figure out the approximate number of guests you can invite. For example, if you've set aside $10,000 just for wedding reception food and drink costs, and you plan on inviting 100 guests, you may book a wedding package priced at $100 a head (taxes, gratuities, and site rental included).

$10,000 available: If 100 guests, then $100 is available to spend per guest

Another way to estimate is to start with a ballpark price per person, which you can get by reviewing menus and catering packages at local banquet halls. For example, lunch at an inexpensive restaurant might come to about $25 per person, whereas a caterer or banquet hall might charge a minimum of $75 per person. Divide the total dollar amount that it will cost you per person into the total amount you have to spend to get a sense of the maximum number of people you may be able to host.

$10,000 available: If 133 guests, then $75 is available to spend per guest

Expect to work and rework the numbers. You may have to cut your list. In talking with the management, for example, ask if the per person price comes with a minimum number of people that you must pay for. Does it include décor, linens, flowers, transportation, service, and the many other items that you'll need? If not, you will have to add the prorated cost of those extras to the total.

Event planning is a complex undertaking, and the larger the event, the more details there are to keep track of. Check out the Party Planning Worksheet on the following pages for tracking the relevant details and to get a reality check about what it takes to throw a sizeable affair. If you get more than one bid for a service, the worksheet has multiple rows under the topic: record additional prices there. It also acts as a ledger. Once you've decided to go with a bid, record the amount in the far right column so you can track how much you're spending. You can copy this worksheet and use the pages for more than one event.

PARTY PLANNING WORKSHEET

This worksheet will help you stay focused and keep track of many details necessary for any successful event. It acts as a ledger as well, so you can also record how much you're spending. Make a copy of these pages if you're planning more than one event.

ITEM	VENDOR NAME & CONTACT INFORMATION	DEADLINE FOR BOOKING	COST	BUDGET TOTAL — AMOUNT SPENT
Initial budget amount				
Location				
Invitations				
Matchbooks				
Printed napkins				
Programs				
Calligraphy				
Maps				
Postage				
Other				

ITEM	VENDOR NAME & CONTACT INFORMATION	DEADLINE FOR BOOKING	COST	BUDGET TOTAL — AMOUNT SPENT
Transportation				
Parking				
Seating chart/placecards/ menu cards				
Food package (appetizer, entrée, dessert)				
Cake				
Candy and sweets				
Alcohol				
Nonalcoholic drinks				

PARTY PLANNING WORKSHEET

ITEM	VENDOR NAME & CONTACT INFORMATION	DEADLINE FOR BOOKING	COST	BUDGET TOTAL — AMOUNT SPENT
Coffee & tea service				
Cooling or heating *(refrigerators, chafing dishes, hot plates, coffee urns)*				
Plates				
Utensils				
Glassware				
Other				

ITEM	VENDOR NAME & CONTACT	DEADLINE FOR BOOKING	COST	BUDGET TOTAL — AMOUNT SPENT
Serving pieces				
(toasting glasses, punchbowl,				
special bowls, trays, tongs,				
forks, cake servers, etc.)				
Tables				
Chairs				
Linens				
Centerpieces				
Room décor				

PARTY PLANNING WORKSHEET

ITEM	VENDOR NAME & CONTACT INFORMATION	DEADLINE FOR BOOKING	COST	BUDGET TOTAL — AMOUNT SPENT
Emcee				
Maitre'd				
Bartender				
Waitstaff, etc.				
(cloakroom attendent,				
parking valet, etc.)				
Clergy				
Decorations				
(Balloons, urns, arches,				
runners, ribbons)				

ITEM	VENDOR NAME & CONTACT INFORMATION	DEADLINE FOR BOOKING	COST	BUDGET TOTAL — AMOUNT SPENT
Cleaning staff				
Cleaning equipment				
Guest book				
Guest amenities				
(soaps, hand lotion, guest				
towels, room spray, etc.)				
Disposable cameras				
and film				
Candles				
Party game supplies				
Favors				
Other				

PARTY PLANNING WORKSHEET

ITEM	VENDOR NAME & CONTACT INFORMATION	DEADLINE FOR BOOKING	COST	BUDGET TOTAL — AMOUNT SPENT
Lighting				
Audio equipment				
Entertainment				
(music, soloists,				
karaoke, DJ)				
Games				
Videography				
Photography				

ITEM	VENDOR NAME & CONTACT INFORMATION	DEADLINE FOR BOOKING	COST	BUDGET TOTAL — AMOUNT SPENT
Clothing				
(wedding gown, shoes,				
tuxedos)				
Beauty services				
(hair, makeup, manicurist,				
pedicurist)				
Jewelry				
Gifts				
Cleaners				
Other				

WEDDING RESOURCES
Mother of the Bride Gowns and Planning Help

We've assembled the following list of resources as an aide for both searching for and buying the "perfect" dress for you, the mother of the bride. As well, we've included planning guides that further assist you in helping to plan a memorable wedding for your daughter.

There are hundreds, if not thousands, of Internet sites that advertise gowns. But buyers who shop for an expensive, possibly special-order gown over the Internet should beware. How do you know if the business is legitimate, or whether it can process your order in time? And even if the online store does ship out a gown to you, what will happen if it does not fit?

There is no simple answer to this question. Manufacturers generally advise buyers to purchase gowns only from authorized retailers. There have been a number of instances where a designer's gown has been knocked off or sold through an unauthorized dealer. Manufacturers will not accept responsibility for a gown unless it was produced by, and purchased through, an authorized dealer.

However, online catalogues can be helpful when it comes to finding out what the current styles are, which designers target the mother of the bride, and which designers are carried by stores in your area — or which stores in your area carry a favorite designer.

On the following pages are the Web sites of some manufacturers who create mother-of-the-bride outfits and special occasion looks. These may offer a starting point for dress and outfit ideas and purchases.

Please note: There are literally hundreds of designers, and the following is just a small sample.

NOTE: The inclusion of a Web site, book, designer, or gown manufacturer here does not constitute an endorsement by the authors of this book.

Alberto Makali

Sexy, trendy clothing for the mother of the bride who has a great figure and wants to show it off. The evening collection features rich colors and bold patterns. The collection is targeted towards the woman who is not afraid to be noticed.
www.albertomakali.com

Alfred Angelo

In business for decades, this manufacturer promises "affordable gowns for every member of the wedding party" in dozens of colors, from size 2 to 28W. There is no specific collection targeted for the mother of the bride, but a number of the designs, which are classic in style, can be worn by her.

The Web site has a "mix and match" section to create your own look by choosing different tops and skirts to create your own wedding-day look.
www.alfredangelo.com

Alex Evenings

This company offers classic styling that should appeal to more conservative mothers. Many of the gowns come in neutral colors and with jackets.
www.alexevenings.com

Adrianna Papell

Known for its prom gowns, this company can be an option for a smaller-size mother of the bride (up to size 14), who wants a glamorous evening look for a relatively inexpensive price.
www.adriannapapell.com

Cameron Blake/Mon Cheri Bridal

Mon Cheri, one of the largest manufacturers of bridal gowns, has a number of collections that may be of interest. Their *Destinations* catalog features special occasion dresses in floaty fabrics suitable for casual affairs. *Montage* offers mother of bride and occasion wear in crepe satins, shantung, and prints. *Mon Cheri Evenings* offers sophisticated eveningwear in crepes, and chiffon. *The Cameron Blake* collection is another line specifically targeted to the mother of the bride, featuring floaty suits and dresses in subtle shades. Depending on the collection, sizes range between 6 and 22.
www.mon-cheri.co.uk

Cassandra Stone

This company offers beauty pageant styling geared towards the prom market, but the gowns are available in plus sizes, too.
www.cassandrastone.com

Daymor

This designer offers a collection of long gowns with jackets in the traditional mother-of-the-bride styling.
www.daymor.com

Jessica McClintock

This designer creates feminine looks with romantic styling that appeals to those with a Victorian sensibility.
www.jessicamcclintock.com

Mike Benet

In the fashion industry for over 45 years, this Texas-based company designs elegant, sophisticated formal gowns for prom, pageant, and special occasion.
www.mikebenetformals.com

Bridal magazines also have Web sites, which can be helpful for general information on planning weddings and online wedding planners.

www.theknot.com
www.brides.com
www.modernbride.com
www.elegantbride.com
www.marthastewart.com

Or, consider one of these traditional wedding planners:

The Bride's Year Ahead: The Ultimate Month-by-Month Wedding Planner by Marguerite Smolen, photographs by Carol Ross
Planning a Wedding to Remember: The Perfect Wedding Planner, Sixth Edition, by Beverly Clark
The Creative Wedding Organizer and Planner by Theresa Chan
Martha Stewart's Keepsake Wedding Planner by Martha Stewart, Janine Nichols
The Knot Ultimate Wedding Planner by Carley Roney
Emily Post's Wedding Planner by Peggy Post

Names & Addresses

_____

_____

_____

_____

_____

_____

_____

_____

_____

_____

_____

Names & Addresses

INDEX

About the Author

Marguerite Smolen has nearly two decades of experience writing about weddings. She began her career in bridal journalism as editorial director of *New Jersey Bride* magazine and then founded the regional magazine, *Philadelphia Bride.*

About the Photographer

Carol Ross's photographs have been published by Simon & Schuster and appear in *Feels Like Home* (Algonquin Books), as well as *The Bride's Year Ahead* published by Sellers Publishing, Inc. Ross, who lives in Bucks County, Pennsylvania, is a well-known wedding photographer.

ISBN 1-56906-578-0